Jewish Liturgy

A Guide for Everyone

Hazzan Abbe Lyons

To all my teachers,
particularly to Rabbi Marcia Prager,
who opened my eyes to the multiplicity of meaning
of each word of Hebrew liturgy,
Rabbi Zalman Schachter-Shalomi,
whose English davennen expanded and deepened
my connection to liturgy,
and Hazzan Jack Kessler
whose assignment to write about liturgy for laypeople
was the first draft of this book.

CONTENTS

The prayer book is our Jewish diary of the centuries, a collection of prayers composed by generations of those who came before us, as they endeavored to express the meaning of their lives. To know the prayer book is to know our history from within. It is to be in touch with the soul of the Jewish people, as it has evolved in good times and in bad, through persecutions and Golden Ages. The Siddur is our encounter with 3,000 years of fate, condensed in a form available to the average Jew, who, today no less than yesterday, may have insufficient time and knowledge to dip deeply into Talmud, Midrash, philosophy and Kabbalah, but who can capture the essence of the Jewish spirit just by reading through the pages of our liturgy.

–Rabbi Lawrence A. Hoffman, *My People's Prayer Book*

WHERE DOES JEWISH LITURGY
COME FROM?

We tend to think of the synagogue service as an ancient rite that we inherited with few changes from Talmudic times, until the Reform movement sparked a modern period of change. In fact, although some basic structures have been handed down to us from late antiquity, Jewish liturgy has been continually evolving.

Where does Jewish liturgy come from?
And how did prayer services begin?

In ancient times, the Israelites developed their cultural, spiritual and religious practice, which included making prescribed offerings and retelling sacred stories, many of which became the core of the Hebrew Bible. In some of the stories, people made food offerings as a way to connect with the community and with G-d, to seek forgiveness or to give thanks. The **Torah**[1] includes detailed descriptions of how food became transformed into sacred offerings. Today we still transform food into sacred offerings by saying blessings over the food on our tables and giving thanks after we have eaten. In some of the stories, people prayed using words: praising, pleading, giving thanks, questioning, repenting.

Today we still pray using words, making regular use of a large body of liturgy found in the prayerbook. However, the people praying with words in the Torah did so spontaneously, not from a pre-composed text, although some of their prayers have become part of

---

[1] **Bold** terms are defined in the glossary on page 23.

our liturgy. Somehow, there was a process from these two modalities – a structured system of offerings combined with spontaneous, individual prayer with no defined structures – to the fully developed communal liturgy of Jewish prayer we have today, in which spontaneous individual prayer is allowed, but often seen as an adjunct to the liturgy. Not only congregations, but also individuals praying on their own are encouraged to use standard liturgy as their basic prayer practice.

HOW THE PRAYERS WERE FORMULATED

In the **Talmud**, which famously begins with a query about when is the appropriate time to recite the evening *Sh'ma*, there are references to prayer, but worship (service to G-d) at the Temple was mainly through the system of food offerings. Outside the Temple, and after the destruction of the Temple, liturgy began to develop as an alternative, and then a substitute for Temple worship. Prayer became a way to worship and to serve G-d, using food blessings and holiday practices in the home, and the worship service (which in modern English we often refer to as "services") in the larger community. However, when the prayer service first began, it was an oral tradition. There was no prayer book, in part because books were not accessible to many people, and there were only hand-copied manuscripts, not bound books printed on a printing press. We see the beginnings of the modern prayer book in the Talmud, where some blessings, prayers and practices are referred to or even specified. Several blessing formulas were established, all beginning with the familiar *Baruch Ata*, Blessed are You:

Blessed are You	*Baruch ata Adonai*	בָּרוּךְ אַתָּה יְיָ
Blessed are You, God our God, who rules all time and space	*Baruch ata Adonai eloheinu melech haOlam*	בָּרוּךְ אַתָּה יְיָ אֱלֹהֵינוּ מֶלֶךְ הָעוֹלָם
Blessed are You, God our God, who rules all time and space, who makes us holy with commandments and commands us	*Baruch ata Adonai eloheinu melech haOlam asher kid'shanu b'mitzvotav v'tzivanu*	בָּרוּךְ אַתָּה יְיָ אֱלֹהֵינוּ מֶלֶךְ הָעוֹלָם אֲשֶׁר קִדְּשָׁנוּ בְּמִצְוֹתָיו וְצִוָּנוּ

It is worth noting that this blessing formula is in the second person, Blessed are You, rather than the third person, Blessed is God. This second person language calls us to be fully present and engaged as we speak blessings. As Rabbi Marcia Prager writes in *The Path of Blessing*:

> Every time I say "you" to my beloved, I speak
> also to God. Every time I say "You" to God, I
> affirm the Presence of that You in every other
> you. I must see God in each face, in each you,
> or I risk treating you as a use-object, an "it."[2]

Also discussed in the Talmud are an order of themes and a custom of sealing each theme with a closing blessing (using the shortest formula above followed by a phrase summing up the theme). However, the full text of the prayers is not laid out, and the prayer leader would improvise on those themes. Rabbi Lawrence A. Hoffman compares early synagogue prayer to jazz, where a familiar melody – a theme – inspires improvisation. Both the jazz improviser and the prayer improviser start out with and keep referring back to the theme but making it a little – or maybe a lot – different each time. Because we often to try to recreate improvisations that were

---

[2]   Prager, Rabbi Marcia, *The Path of Blessing* (New, York, NY: Bell Tower, 1998), p. 63.

particularly inspiring, and because we are often comforted by familiar routines, a flexible framework can often develop into something firmer, Tradition with a capital T. This is referred to in the Talmud as **keva** (fixed, predictable order). We also have a desire to innovate and experience something new and inspiring, and to infuse even familiar routines with vitality and sincerity. This is referred to in the Talmud as **kavvanah** (intention, inspiration, "inner directedness of the heart"[3]). In the Talmud, and in Jewish communities since the Talmud, there is not agreement on which is the greatest priority: *keva or kavvanah,* or if it is important to find a balance.

Within the Talmud, the rabbis debated over the *keva* of synagogue prayer, and eventually a variety of rules regarding communal prayer practice were generally accepted, including who should gather to pray, when to pray, and what to pray about. However, there were still plenty of details left up to the community and its prayer leaders.

Some prayers were direct quotes from the **Tanach** and even later Jewish texts, including the first line of the *Shema* and the paragraph which follows it beginning with *V'ahavta.* Some prayers were composed and shaped by oral tradition, we do not know their authors, but they often include brief quotes or paraphrases from Tanach that fit the theme. There is also a long tradition of religious hymns, called **piyyutim** and **pizmonim**, which were composed and added into the prayer service. They were not considered essential, but some have become so common that many people know them as well or even better than some of the original essential prayers, though their authorship is not always known. *Ein Keloheinu, Adon Olam,* and *L'cha dodi* are some well-known and much beloved piyyutim. There are also many *piyyutim* that were written for specific holidays, especially High Holidays, such as *Unetaneh tokef,* which was probably written in by an early hymn composer (**paytan**) but was later attributed to Rabbi Amnon of Mainz as part of a story of martyrdom.[4]

---

3   Hoffman, *Prayer Book: Vol.1 – Sh'ma,* p. 3.

4   Yahalom, Yosef, "Who shall be the author, and who shall not," *Haaretz,* December 31, 2009 Tevet 14, 5770, http://www.haaretz.com/hasen/pages/ShArt.jhtml?itemNo=205597

TWO MAIN SECTIONS…

After the Babylonian exile, the Jewish community split into two communities, one in Babylon and one in Palestine. These two communities began to develop some regional differences, but as recorded in the Talmud both eventually agreed that the service had two main sections: ***Sh'ma uvirchoteha*** (specific Biblical passages with blessings before and afterwards based on specific themes) and the **Amidah** (also known as the *Sh'moneh Esrei* ("Eighteen" Benedictions) or *haT'fillah* ("the Prayer"), a standing prayer that developed into a sequence of specific themes in a certain order, with as few as seven and as many as nineteen components, each considered a benediction or ***b'racha***). The themes and order of these components of the service are discussed at length in Tractate *B'rachot* in the Babylonian Talmud.

Sh'ma uvirchoteha (*Sh'ma* and her blessings)[5]

1. Blessing on creation: *Maariv Aravim* (evening) or *Yotzer Or* (morning)
2. Blessing on Divine love and the gift of the Torah: *Ahavah Raba/Ahavat Olam*
3. The Sh'ma (three paragraphs of Biblical passages)
4. Truth and Redemption: *Emet, Mi Chamocha* (includes Biblical quote)
5. Protection at night: *Hashkivenu*, only said in the evening service.

---

[5] As Hebrew is a gendered language, *Sh'ma uvirchoteha*, which is in feminine gender, is often translated into English as "*Sh'ma* and its blessings," including in the sources cited in this chapter. Because of the prevalence of masculine gender in much of the liturgy, I have chosen to use the feminine gender in this one instance, while also appreciating the gender neutral "its" used elsewhere in the book.

Shema and Its Blessings-evening version

Shema and Its Blessings-themes

Shema and Its Blessings-evening and morning

Barchu   Coming together to pray/praise, minyan

Maariv Aravim (evening) *Yotzer Or (morning)*   Creation, differentiation, cosmos, light & dark

Ahavat Olam/Unending Love (evening) *Ahava Raba/Abundant Love (morning)* Love, the Gift of Torah

Shema – V'ahavta (Torah quote)   the Unity of Diversity the Oneness of the Many Hearing/Here-ing

Emet   Truth - connects two Torah quotes Shema & Mi Chamocha

Mi Chamocha (Torah quote)   Liberation, Redemption, Freedom, Celebration

Hashkivenu (evening ONLY)   Protection, Shelter

Amidah (Standing)/*HaT'fillah* (The Prayer)/*Sh'moneh Esrei* (Eighteen)

Setting an intention: *S'fatai Tiftach* – Open my lips (psalm 51:17)

Opening segment:
1. *Avot* Remembrance of Abraham, Isaac & Jacob and their close relationship to G-d. In some contemporary prayerbooks, *Avot v'Imahot* includes Sarah, Rebecca, Leah and Rachel and their close relationship to G-d
2. *Gvurot* G-d's power of life and death and the changing seasons
3. *Kedushah* G-d's holiness

Middle segment:
One blessing for the holiness of Shabbat or holidays, or thirteen petitions on weekdays for insight, healing, prosperity, etc.

Closing segment:
1. *Avodah* Our prayer is our service to G-d, since we can't bring offerings to the Temple
2. *Hoda'ah* Gratitude
3. *Shalom* A wish for peace and well-being

Add Your Own Personal Prayers or use *Elohai n'tzor* - keep my tongue from evil
Transition - *Yihiyu leratzon* - May my prayers be acceptable (psalm 19:15)
Transition - *Oseh Shalom* - additional request for peace

Amidah-themes

…AND SO MUCH MORE!

These fixed prayers are the essence of liturgy. Yet modern prayer books contain so much more – where did it all come from? Coming out of an improvisation-based oral tradition with varying local and regional customs, wanting both order (*keva*) and novelty (*kavvanah*) are some of the factors that may have led to the prayer book getting longer and longer. Individuals and communities in different generations sought to connect with the meanings of the fixed prayers, and this led them to make changes to the liturgy, either by composing new prayers, revising existing prayers, adding selections from the Bible, Talmud, and *Zohar*, or repeating prayers, such as the *chatzi kaddish*. So many Jews have been inspired to make their own additions to the fixed liturgy that a wealth of amazing material has accumulated over the years, and quite a bit has become "traditional." Modern progressive prayer books, using both Hebrew and English, often delete some of this extra material to keep services from being too long, but then add newly composed prayers or poetry in Hebrew or English.

Along with the blessings of *Sh'ma uvirchoteha* and the *Amidah*, other prayers had been composed, but did not become part of the fixed prayers until later. The *Kaddish* was originally used to honor teachers after text study, but eventually developed into different forms used for other purposes, such as making a transition between sections of the service, and for mourning. *Aleinu* was originally composed specifically for Rosh Hashanah, but gradually became added to all services. In fact, a whole tradition of composing *piyyutim* (liturgical poems) arose sometime around the 4th century. Often *piyyutim* were added around the *Yotzer* and the *Kedusha* prayers in the morning service, but they were also composed for holidays and specific Torah portions. Some of the early *piyyutim* were adopted widely and are still used today, although they were often set to different melodies. Two of the most familiar are *Ein Keloheinu,* which is mentioned in early written versions of the prayer book, and *Adon Olam*, which appears in the medieval period, though it may have been composed earlier.[6] Some of these *piyyutim* spread widely and became part of the liturgy. The best example of this is *L'cha dodi*, one of the most recent additions to the liturgy. Another addition to the service, public reading from the Torah and from the Prophets (*haftarah*) began in ancient times, but the liturgy we use today for Torah services seems to have developed over time. In the Tanach, Nechemyah chapter 8 describes a public Torah reading by Ezra.

---

[6]   See articles on these and other prayers and *piyyutim* in *Encyclopedia Judaica* (Jerusalem: Keter Publishing House, 1971).

THE FIRST ACTUAL PRAYERBOOKS

Beginning in the 8th century, the Jewish world looked to the Babylonian academies of Sura and Pumbedita, whose chief rabbis used the title **Gaon** (plural, *Geonim*). Far-flung Jewish communities began seeking guidance from the Geonim, who disseminated their rulings as if they had authority over all Jewish communities. Natronai Gaon, in response to a Spanish congregation, authored a four page *"siddur"* (from the same root as *seder*, meaning order) which outlined the names and sometimes the closing phrase, known as the **chatima** or "seal" of each blessing a person should say in both public and private worship.[7] His successor, Amram Gaon, in the late 9th century, took the audacious step of writing the *Seder Rav Amram*, which also includes the text of the prayers, which had never before been written down to this extent. This began to be copied and distributed and gained authority as a proper prayer book. Still, there was lots of local and regional variation, especially in Palestine, where the community looked to their own authorities rather than the Geonim in Babylonia. Other prayer books followed, some of which still exist in manuscript or have even been preserved and published, so that scholars of liturgy have been able to compare the variations or "rites" that arose in different regions, many of which are still actively practiced today. The word **nusach** is sometimes used to describe these regional variations, although in addition to the liturgical text, it can also refer to the improvisatory musical modes and motives used by the **hazzan** (cantor), rabbi or prayer leader for specific days or times of day, which also vary by region. Some prayerbooks specify "Nusach Sephardi" or "Nusach Ashkenaz" to indicate that they are

---

[7]   Elbogen, Ismar, *Jewish Liturgy: A Comprehensive History* (Philadelphia: Jewish Publication Society, 1993), §43:4, p. 275.

generally following the liturgical customs and texts used in many Sephardi or many Ashkenazi communities, but there are many more specific *nuscha'ot* such as Spanish-Portuguese, Italian, Catalonian, German, Eastern European, Alsatian, Yemeni, Baghdadi, Moroccan, Algerian, Turkish, Indian, and many more, each with their own prayerbook.

The invention of the printing press in the fifteenth century caused more uniformity and less variety, although melodies, *piyyutim* and detailed customs still vary significantly in different regional traditions. Rabbi Lawrence Hoffman notes that "Jewish liturgy has never recovered from the onslaught of the printing press."[8] Once prayer books could be printed, everyone had the same text, and improvisation was more likely to be found in melody (*hazzanut*) or in new *piyyutim*.

Although the printing press helped prayer books go viral, the internet and social media have taken this to a new level. Despite the improvisatory roots of our liturgical tradition and the authority that each local community has to determine - and change - its own liturgical **minhag** (custom), the internet has allowed claims to what is "authentic" or "original" to vie for search engine optimization. Simultaneously the digital environment has encouraged tremendous variation and creativity. Jewish liturgy is an ongoing process!

---

[8] Hoffman, *Prayer Book: Vol.1 – Sh'ma*, p. 10.

THE INFLUENCE OF KABBALAH

In medieval times, the mystical tradition gave rise to **Kabbalah**, which has had a profound influence on the synagogue service and on ideas about prayer, from the Hasidei Ashkenaz in 12th century Germany to the Kabbalists in Provence and Spain in the 13th century,[9] when the *Zohar* was first published, peaking with the Safed kabbalists led by Rabbi Isaac Luria ("the Ari") in the 16th century, and continuing through the Hassidic movements.

In Kabbalistic thought, proper intention (*Kavvanah*) was seen as a way towards redemption of the Jewish people. Proper *Kavvanah* would help the mystic focus his prayer to achieve full spiritual concentration. The mystic endeavor was to become a kind of spiritual superhero. This could make a *tikkun* (repair) in the sefirotic world, to return the Shechinah and/or the people of Israel from exile. Written *Kavvanot*, meditations or selections from scripture or from the *Zohar* were added to kabbalistically influenced prayerbooks so that the worshipper could use the appropriate *kavvanah*. The prayers themselves, as well as the gestures and body movements of prayer, began to take on new mystical meanings. This strengthened not only *kavvanah* but also *keva*, since

> "…the very fact that [the printing press] could
> etch particular words as if in stone lent credence
> to the mystics' claim that every word mattered
> to the point where changing a single vowel
> might ruin the secret message of a prayer."[10]

---

[9] Steinsalz, Rabbi Adin, *A Guide to Jewish Prayer* (New York: Schocken books, 2000), p. 59.

[10] Hoffman, *Prayer Book: Vol.1 – Sh'ma*, p. 10.

Shabbat and holidays gave the Spanish and later the Safed kabbalists extra opportunities to increase heavenly balance and earthly redemption. The Safed kabbalists were inspired by the Babylonian Talmud Shabbat 119a, in which R. Hanina welcomed the Sabbath queen and R. Jannai welcomed the Sabbath bride. This led them to develop of the Kabbalat Shabbat service,[11] their most drastic and far-reaching alteration on the synagogue service. This was accepted and remains part of the liturgy in some form in most Jewish communities all over the world.[12] It is astonishing that this addition from the 16th century has become as entrenched as the *Sh'ma* and *Amidah*, which are so much older and more grounded in early Judaic traditions. The image of welcoming Shabbat as a queen or a bride seems to captivate people of different genders, in congregations belonging to all parts of the spectrum of Jewish practice. Even those who disdain mysticism would not delete Rabbi Shlomo Alkabetz's well-beloved *piyyut, Lecha dodi*, from the Friday evening service.

The ideas and practices of the Safed Kabbalists exerted a tremendous influence on the wider Jewish community. Joseph Karo was both legal scholar and kabbalist, and his *Shulchan Arukh* is still considered a primary, essential *halakhic* source.[13] The kabbalistic idea that redemption will come only with our efforts in proper prayer practices and the observance of all commands, or **mitzvot**, from the Bible as interpreted in the Talmud,[14] has had and is still having an effect on many diverse Jewish communities. Hasidism embraced and, to a certain extent, popularized kabbalah, which influenced even those who opposed Hasidism's devotional, mystical, populist message.

The rise of Hasidism in the 18th century served to make Lurianic and other kabbalistic ideas more accessible. Its founder, the Baal Shem Tov, taught that "every true prayer has the power to influence the

---

[11]   See Scherman, Rabbi Nosson, *Complete Artscroll Siddur: Nusach Sefard* (Brooklyn: Mesorah Publications, 1985), p. 350, and Fine, Lawrence, *Safed Spirituality – Rules of Mystical Piety, the Beginning of Wisdom* (Mahwah: Paulist Press, 1984), p. 33.

[12]   Elbogen, *Liturgy*, §15:2, p. 92.

[13]   Fine, Lawrence, *Physician of the Soul, Healer of the Cosmos: Isaac Luria and His Kabbalistic Fellowship* (Stanford: Stanford University Press, 2003), p. 54, and Steinsalz, *Guide*, p. 417.

[14]   Fine, *Safed Spirituality*, pp. 9-10.

upper realms"[15] and that ecstatic prayer is essential to become closer to God and to bring the people of Israel closer to redemption. Many Hasidim prayed loudly and enthusiastically, with singing, dancing, even somersaults. Hasidic masters such as R. Levi Yitzhak of Berditchev became famous for their *hitlahavut*, or "burning enthusiasm," in prayer,[16] even some, like R. Abraham of Slonim, whose *hitlahavut* took the subtler form of tremendous stillness.[17] They used every aspect of prayer (words, wordless melodies, movements, visual images through stories) as a way to induce ecstatic trance-like experiences. In a way, they foreshadowed the ideas of modern educators who argue that not everyone learns or even senses the world in the same way, and that involving multiple kinds of stimuli (visual, auditory and kinesthetic) can make learning not only accessible, but also richer for more and more people, which may explain the appeal of Hasidic prayer.

---

[15]   Elbogen, *Liturgy*, §44:8, p. 294.

[16]   Jacobs, Louis, *Hasidic Prayer* (London: Littman Library of Jewish Civilization, 1972), p. 94.

[17]   Jacobs, *Hasidic Prayer*, p. 63.

MODERN DIVISIONS

In Europe, tremendous political and social changes had a major effect on Jewish communities. By the mid-19th century, Jews in many European nation-states were emancipated and given citizenship, and it became possible for Jews to assimilate without converting to Christianity. More Jews were exposed to philosophy and literature as well as Torah and Talmud. The Reform movement began with liturgical reform. A group of modern-minded Jews in Hamburg began to worship using a shortened service, with prayers in not only in Hebrew but also in German (their everyday language), with some small, but significant, changes in Hebrew prayers. They also introduced choirs and organs and sermons in German. The Hamburg Prayer book created an uproar among the rabbinate when it was first published in 1819, and again with the second edition in 1841.[18] Although these reforms were not random and the reformers consulted the Talmud and other rabbinic sources to ground their reforms in Jewish law, a Jewish counter-reformation arose in protest, which became the modern Orthodox movement. In 1845 a progressive rabbi, Zacharias Frankel, felt the reformers were going too far and broke away to found the modern Conservative movement. All these streams of Judaism published multiple prayer-books and began to develop different worship styles. Liturgy was one of several significant factors in how these movements began to define themselves.

Liturgy, especially in Ashkenazic communities, has continued to evolve in the twentieth century, both in text and in style. Various Reform, Conservative and Orthodox prayer books have been

---

[18]   Petuchowski, J.J., "Reform Judaism," *Encyclopedia Judaica* (Jerusalem: Keter Publishing House, 1971), Volume 14, p. 23.

published, each with its own clarifications reflecting the theology and practices. In the Sephardic world, including Jewish communities in the Middle East and Eretz Yisrael, liturgical practice has been subject to less upheaval, though some important regional differences can be seen in different prayer books. New *piyyutim* continue to be composed which add to an already rich tradition, enhancing all sorts of services, gatherings and life cycle events. Progressive Judaism has been influenced by Sephardic practice, adopting the Sephardic-style pronunciation of modern Hebrew[19] for prayer as well as conversation, and Reform liturgists have drawn on Sephardic as well as Ashkenazi liturgy.

As in Europe in the nineteenth century, in the United States in the 20th century, Ashkenazi liturgy has changed, especially among progressive Jewish communities. In the 1940s, a new movement – Jewish Reconstructionism, was founded by Rabbi Mordecai Kaplan, and his prayer book was published. Beginning in the 1960s, influenced by the counterculture in the US and the UK, some Jews were inspired to experiment with new forms of Jewish worship community, such as *chavurot* and independent *minyanim*, new styles of Jewish liturgical music and new attitudes toward liturgy, especially valuing *kavvanah* over *keva*. Two rabbis who came out of the Hasidic world, Rabbis Shlomo Carlebach and Zalman Schachter-Shalomi, combined this spirit of experimentation and openness with their firm grounding in and extensive knowledge of Jewish texts, liturgy, and prayer practices, exerting a tremendous influence while also encouraging others to learn more and grow into leadership. Out of this experimentation came the Havurah movement and the Jewish Renewal movement. Service leaders designed creative services based on the structure of the fixed prayers, using a combination of Hebrew and English, seeking to express the themes of the prayers through text, melody, movement, storytelling, guided meditation and imagery. The influence of feminism and women becoming rabbis and cantors has influenced liturgy, to the extent that the first blessing

---

[19] As with other languages, there are regional and subgroup differences in pronunciation rules, which can change both the default accents and the pronunciation of certain vowels and consonants. The word *mitzvot*, for instance, can be pronounced *MITZ-ves* in Ashkenazi-Yiddish pronunciation, or *mitz-VOT* in Sephardi pronunciation; similarly, the word *g'veret* will be pronounced *g'VEH-ret* by modern Israeli speakers but as *ja-BAH-rath* by traditional Yemeni Jews.

of the *T'filah*, *Avot* (Patriarchs) is now *Avot v'Imahot* (Patriarchs and Matriarchs) in most progressive prayer books. Ashkenazi Jews have become more aware of Sephardic and Mizrachi liturgical and musical traditions. *Nigunnim*, or wordless melodies, which were used extensively in Hasidic communities in Eastern Europe, were used to activate various devotional states, both inward and celebratory, and even to activate certain spiritual teachings. While some Hasidic *nigunnim* were quite brilliantly composed, they were not intended for performance or passive listening, but to evoke spiritual states through participatory singing. Either without words, or with just a phrase or two, *nigunnim* were intended to focus one's *kavvanah* rather than go through the entire liturgical text. Schachter-Shalomi and Carlebach helped spread this kind of participatory, communal Jewish music of short texts or syllables (such as *yai dai dai*) all over the United States. Carlebach's *V'ha-eir eineinu* and *Esa Einai*, among others, are well known in Orthodox and Conservadox as well as liberal communities.

All these factors have resulted in tremendous creativity, not only in liberal congregations but throughout the Jewish world, particularly in the United States. Interest in the many layers of meaning embedded in Hebrew liturgical texts has led to new translations, new prayerbooks and new understandings of the prayers. Once again, Jewish liturgy is enriched by the dance between *keva* and *kavvanah*. We have a treasure trove of Jewish liturgical creativity. The Jewish people are still inspired to continue – and preserve – our conversations with and about G-d.

GLOSSARY

Amidah – collection of 19 benedictions recited while standing in each of the 3 daily services (from the Hebrew, "to stand")

B'racha – blessing or benediction (from the Hebrew, "to bless")

Chatima – the closing sentence of a prayer, usually using the blessing formula "Blessed are You, G-d [phrase about the theme of the prayer]" (from the Hebrew "to seal")

Gaon (plural, *geonim*) – Title used for the chief rabbis of the Babylonian academies of Sura and Pumbedita in the 7th - 11th centuries, who were widely recognized throughout the Jewish world as authorities on Jewish law and custom.

Hazzan/Hazzanut – Hazzan, from the root for vision, is the Hebrew title for the cantor. In early synagogues the hazzan had more of a day-to-day organizational role, but later the title hazzan was used to denote a skilled prayer leader.
Hazzanut is a term for the musical material used by the hazzan, which can include *nusach* (used for liturgical text), cantillation or trope (used for public readings from Torah, haftarah and *megillot*), as well as folk or composed melodies (used for *piyyutim* and sometimes for prayers).

Kabbalah – most famous stream of Jewish mysticism (from the Hebrew "to receive") and its texts and practices. The Zohar is the most famous Kabbalistic text.

Kavvanah – intention, inspiration, spiritual focus.
Often contrasted with *keva*.

Keva – fixed, predictable order. In the Talmud, the specific liturgical themes, language and choreography for prayer services. Can also refer to what any given community or prayerbook defines as the "rules" for prayer, or "how we do it," which may be based on a halachic (Jewish legal) tradition or on customs that have become community standards.

Often contrasted with *kavvanah*.

Midrash – a rabbinic tradition of embellishing and interpreting Biblical text through imaginative storytelling, drawing a connection between different Biblical texts or between text and practice, and sometimes using word play or even current events. When the text does not fill in all the details, a question is raised by the text, or simply contains an intriguing phrase, there is often a midrash (or more than one) to elaborate, explain, fill in the back story, or offer a completely new interpretation that appears to be unrelated or even opposed to the surface meaning.

Midrash can be in many forms including prose (the most common), poetry, music, visual art or performance art.

Minhag – custom. The customs, or habits, of any given Jewish community, or even the wider community within which a Jewish community is situated. *Minhag* can in many instances affect, or even override, what is considered permitted under Jewish law (*halachah*), including liturgical practices.

Mitzvah (Plural, *mitzvot*) – from the Hebrew root צו, meaning command. Literally means "commandments" but can be understood as instructions or acts of connection.

Nusach – this term is used in two different ways: text-based and melody-based.

1. Text: *Nusach* can be translated as "rite" or "ritual" which refers to variations in the text of the prayers, either broad categories such as Nusach Ashkenaz, Nusach Sephard, Nusach Edot HaMizrach, or to specific regional variations or subdivisions. These include, for instance, "Nusach Catalunya," "the German rite," or "the Morrocan rite" (which also has its own subdivisions). Sometimes the term *Minhag* (custom) is used interchangeably, as in "Minhag Polin" (Eastern European subdivision of Nusach Ashkenaz).

2. Melody: the melodic modes and motives used in chanting sections of liturgical text in a semi-improvisatory fashion. Some modes are used only on certain holidays, while others are used for Shabbat and weekdays. Different modes are used for different sections of the service. In some settings, it might be possible for a person walking into a service to identify the section of

the service or the time of year, just by the melody that is being used

Paytan – a person who writes text or music for piyyutim, or who performs piyyutim (in some traditions, this includes improvisation).

P'ticha – the opening phrase of a prayer (from the Hebrew "to open"), often using the blessing formulas "Blessed are You" or "Blessed are You,, G-d, our G-d, Ruler of the Universe"

Piyyut (plural, *piyyutim*) – liturgical poem or hymn which is sung, chanted or recited during worship services. Piyyutim often use acrostics where the first letter of each line spells out the Hebrew alphabet, the name of the author, a name of G-d or a Hebrew word of religious significance. Some texts have inspired multiple musical settings. (Used in Hebrew, from the Greek, "poet").

Pizmon (plural, *pizmonim*) – Sephardic tradition of songs similar to piyyutim, but usually with the intention of teaching outside of worship and not included in prayer books, often using acrostics (see *piyyut*).

Sh'ma uvirchoteha – *Sh'ma* and her blessings, a section of the Jewish morning and evening prayer services consisting of a series of benedictions, two before and two or three after the *Sh'ma*.

Sh'ma – Three paragraphs of text from the Torah, recited morning and evening. Sometimes used to mean just the first line, which is an affirmation of the Oneness of the Divine, central to Jewish liturgy, thought and practice. The text is included in *mezuzot* ("write them on the doorposts of your house") and *t'fillin* ("a sign upon your hand and frontlets between your eyes."

Talmud – also known as "Oral Law" or "Oral Torah" to indicate that it came after the Written Law (Torah/ Hebrew Bible) and was only passed down orally through a tradition of memorization, not committed to writing. An enormous collection of teachings, interpretations, and expansions of the Hebrew Bible, composed mostly after the 1st and 2nd Temples were destroyed. The Talmud includes debates and discussions by the early rabbinic sages on law, ethics, business, spiritual and religious practice including *mitzvot* (commandments/ obligations from the Hebrew Bible), and every aspect of daily life, as well as midrash (legends and stories).

Tanach or **TaNaKh** – an acronym referring to the three sections of the Hebrew Bible: Torah, Prophets and Writings (**T**orah, **N**'vi'im, **K**'tuvim). These are the primary Jewish canonical texts, all of which were originally written in Hebrew. Also known as the Written Torah, because the text characterizes itself as being written down, in contrast with the Mishnah and Talmud, known as the Oral Torah, since they came from an oral tradition which spanned several centuries before being considered complete enough to write down

Torah – Five Books of Moses (first 5 books of the Hebrew Bible); also, a handwritten parchment scroll containing those books; also used to refer to Jewish texts and teachings as a whole, since all Jewish texts and teachings all refer back to the Hebrew Bible and especially the first 5 books. From the Hebrew, meaning instruction, law, in archery: the process of aiming the arrow.
Also known as "Written Law."

BIBLIOGRAPHY

Elbogen, Ismar, *Jewish Liturgy: A Comprehensive History* (Philadelphia: Jewish Publication Society, 1993).

Encyclopedia Judaica (Jerusalem: Keter Publishing House, 1971).

Fine, Lawrence, *Physician of the Soul, Healer of the Cosmos: Isaac Luria and His Kabbalistic Fellowship* (Stanford: Stanford University Press, 2003).

Fine, Lawrence, *Safed Spirituality – Rules of Mystical Piety, the Beginning of Wisdom* (Mahwah: Paulist Press, 1984).

Green, Arthur, *A Guide to the Zohar* (Stanford: Stanford University Press, 2004).

Hoffman, Rabbi Lawrence A., ed., *My People's Prayer Book: Volume 1 – The Sh'ma and Its Blessings* (Woodstock, VT: Jewish Lights Publishing, 1997).

Hoffman, Rabbi Lawrence A., ed., *My People's Prayer Book: Volume 2 – The Amidah* (Woodstock, VT: Jewish Lights Publishing, 1998).

Hoffman, Rabbi Lawrence A., *The Canonization of the Synagogue Service* (Notre Dame: University of Notre Dame Press, 1979).

Jacobs, Louis, *Hasidic Prayer* (London: Littman Library of Jewish Civilization, 1972).

Prager, Rabbi Marcia, *The Path of Blessing* (New York, NY: Bell Tower, 1998).

Schäfer, Peter, *Hekhalot-Studien* (Tübingen: J.C.B.Mohr).

Scherman, Rabbi Nosson, *Complete Artscroll Siddur: Nusach Sefard* (Brooklyn: Mesorah Publications, 1985).

Scholem, Gershom, *Major Trends in Jewish Mysticism* (New York: Shocken Books, 1941).

Steinsalz, Rabbi Adin, *A Guide to Jewish Prayer* (New York: Schocken books, 2000).

ABOUT THE AUTHOR

Hazzan Abbe Lyons is dedicated to making Jewish music, learning and practice both accessible and inspiring, in everyday life as well as at sacred times. She is on the faculty at ALEPH Ordination Programs, where she studied with Hazzan Jack Kessler and received *s'micha* as Hazzan (Cantor) in 2010. She is the Jewish Chaplain for Hillel at Ithaca College, where she received a B.Mus. in voice performance in 1987. She has also worked as a somatic educator and in the nonprofit sector, including Hillel at Binghamton.

Hazzan Lyons is a writer and innovative liturgist whose published work includes poetry and alternative social justice *haftarot*. In 2017 she and her multifaith band, Resonate, released the album, *Listen!* Other recording credits include *Behold!* (Vocolot, 1997), *Roots and Wings* (Vocolot, 1992) and *Household Chores* (Abbe Lyons, 1990). In 2005, she was honored as a Bat Kol, an emerging voice, and in 2022 as an Eshet Hazon, a Woman of Vision. As a SpeakChorus Torah Project educator, she has facilitated SpeakChorus Torah at Ruach HaAretz retreat, the ALEPH Kallah, and in congregational settings with adults and teens.